Action Sports Library

MOTOCROSS

Bob Italia

Published by Abdo & Daughters, 6535 Cecilia Circle, Edina, Minnesota 55439.

Library bound edition distributed by Rockbottom Books, Pentagon Tower, P.O. Box 36036, Minneapolis, Minnesota 55435.

Printed in the United States.

Library of Congress Cataloging-in-Publication Data

Italia, Robert, 1955-
        Motocross / written by Bob Italia.
                p.   cm -- (Action sports)
        Includes bibliographical references (p.   ) and index.
        ISBN 1-56239-233-6
        1. Motocross -- Juvenile literature. I. Title. II Series: Action sports
(Edina, Minn.)
GV1062.12.I83 1993
796.7'56 -- dc20   93 19140
                                                           CIP
                                                           AC

Cover Photo: Allsport.
Inside Photos: Allsport 4, 8, 11, 12, 14, 15, 17, 19, 20, 23, 24, 29, 30.
                 Bettman 6.
                 SportsChrome 26.

Warning: The series *Action Sports Library* is intended as entertainment for children. These sporting activities should never be attempted without the proper conditioning, training, instruction, supervision, and equipment.

Edited by Rosemary Wallner

CONTENTS

Motocross is the most exciting sport on two wheels.

MOTOCROSS

Cross-country Motorcycling—Motocross!

Motocross is the most exciting and challenging sport on two wheels. It combines the raw power of motorcycling with the thrills and obstacles of cross-country racing.

Motocross riders must race over hills, jump ravines, climb hills, and twist around treacherous turns on their roaring mechanized bikes. But motocross is more than racing around a dirt track on a motorcycle. This fast-paced sport demands physical fitness, lightning reflexes, carefully honed riding skills, and lots of practice. Motocross also rewards its participants with lots of outrageous fun.

Looking for New Thrills

Motocross began in 1924 in Surrey, England, shortly after the motorcycle was invented. Motorcycle enthusiasts of the Camberly Club were looking for new ways to enjoy their strange and thrilling mechanical beasts. They laid out a 30-mile dirt course with two steep hills and a three-mile-long straightaway.

The racers wore cloth caps, riding breeches, full-length storm coats, and thick scarfs. They were required to cover two laps—one in the morning and one in the afternoon. The fastest overall time was the winner. Suddenly, "motocross" (cross-country motorcycling) was born.

The early days of motocross.

Motocross did not catch on internationally until after World War II. That's when great strides were made in motocross bike manufacturing. Improvements like the telescopic front fork revolutionized the suspension systems. The telescopic front fork acts like a shock absorber. It enables the cyclist to withstand the great pounding on the motocross track.

Early motocross bikes were big, powerful, and heavy—not like today's quick, light, and agile bikes. Lighter, faster motocross bikes did not appear until the mid 1960s.

Then, in 1968, the Japanese manufacturer Suzuki changed the face of the sport. Suzuki began building motocross bikes on a large scale. Now the fast, rugged, lightweight bikes—made of titanium and aluminum alloy—were available to more and more people. Motocross became more popular than ever. Motocross courses sprouted up everywhere.

That same year, the Trans-AMA series was started in the United States. What began as an event to promote the sale of motorcycles has now blossomed into a motocross event that attracts the best riders in America. Today, motocross remains one of the world's most thrilling and challenging sports.

Choosing a Bike

Buying a motocross bike can be just as thrilling as running your first race. But it is important to select the type of bike that complements a rider's abilities.

Engine capacity is the first factor to consider. Most motocross bikes come with 125cc, 250cc, and 500cc engines. Typically, the larger the engine, the greater the power. If you are a beginner, experts recommend the 250cc bike. Here's why.

The 125cc bike is light and quick. But it requires the rider to keep the engine revved continuously. This makes the bike difficult to handle.

If you are a beginner, experts recommend
the 250cc motocross bike.

High-revving engines are also expensive to maintain. They wear quickly and easily. Engine parts often need replacing.

The 500cc bikes are big and powerful, but they are hard to maneuver. They can attain a high speed in seconds, but all this power makes jumps and turns difficult. There are few professional racers who can handle them with ease. In the hands of a beginner, the 500cc bike would cause many accidents.

The 250cc bikes offer a blend of the 125cc's lightweight maneuverability and the 500cc's power. The 250 can be revved like a 125, or zoom down a straightaway like a 500. Most importantly, the 250 is a sturdy, long-lasting bike that is easy to ride. It does not require any special knowledge or skills. These qualities make the 250 an ideal bike for the motocross beginner.

When buying a bike, the second most important factor are the tires. Motocross tires come in three types: hard terrain, soft terrain, and intermediate.

Hard terrain tires have small knobbles or lugs. These lugs give the tire its gripping power. Soft terrain tires have larger lugs for extra gripping power. Intermediate tires fall between hard and soft terrain tires. Most motocross bikes come equipped with intermediate tires. These offer the best traction for beginners.

Taking Care of a Motocross Bike

After you choose a motocross bike, it is important to take care of it. Having all the riding talent in the world won't help if your equipment fails.

Repairing motocross bikes can be expensive. But if you take care of your bike, repair costs can be kept at a minimum. The air filter should be cleaned often, and oil should be changed regularly.

Keeping your bike clean is just as important as regular maintenance. When you're done riding for the day, resist the urge to leave the dirty bike in the garage till the next day. This gives the mud a chance to harden—and make the cleaning even tougher.

Wrap some plastic around the exhaust pipe and carburetor. Take the garden hose and clean the bike, using the spray nozzle. Use a stiff brush to remove most of the mud. To avoid damage and scratches, use a softer brush for the brakes, tank, and wheels. For a gleaming shine, wipe the bike with a sponge dipped in soapy water, then rinse off the bike.

It's important to keep a motocross bike clean.

When you're finished washing the bike, dry the chain and spray it with lubricant. Dry the wheels so the hubs and brakes won't rust. Finally, spray the entire bike with water repellant. This prevents rust from developing, and makes it harder for mud to cling to the bike.

Riding Gear

Of all the riding gear available, the most important is the helmet. Experts recommend that you buy a helmet from a well-known and respected manufacturer. These helmets are more expensive—but worth it.

A full-faced helmet with goggles.

The best helmets are made of fiberglass. They resist chipping and scratching. They are not affected by gasoline or harmful solvents. And they can easily be resprayed to extend product life. Most importantly, good helmets are certified by the Safety Helmet Council of America (SHCA). Only certified helmets are allowed in motocross competition events.

Make sure the helmet is *full faced*. A full-faced helmet has a face guard bolted on. Helmets with clip-on face guards do not offer the same protection. The clip-on face guards tend to come off in accidents, and offer little protection against flying debris.

The helmet should fit snugly. In the event of an accident, a snug-fitting helmet absorbs the shock. It also provides a more comfortable ride. And it won't rattle around while the rider encounters the more difficult stretches of the motocross course.

An equally important addition to the helmet are goggles. Choose a brand that is designed for motocross. The goggles should be wide and comfortable. They should also have a wide band that will not slip on the helmet.

The best goggle lenses are scratch resistant. Tear-off sheets can also be attached to them. Tear-offs are thin plastic covers fitted to the lense. As many as five can be stacked on top of each other. When one tear-off gets muddy, the rider removes the sheet with one hand, leaving a clean tear-off beneath.

Boots are another important motocross accessory. Plastic boots were once popular. But leather has proven to be the best for flexibility, strength, and wear.

Boots are another important accessory.

Boots should be firm fitting and always strapped up tight. Look for boots with drawstrings. The strings pull the boot tight onto the rider's leg. They are a big safety factor.

A good boot also has a barred sole. Slipper (smooth) soles were once popular. They allowed the boot to slide over the ground without snagging. But their smooth surfaces made it nearly impossible to push a bike on the dirt. The barred sole does not snag the ground. It gives you good traction when needed.

Make sure the boots offer shin protection. This includes a thick layer of polythene backed by solid foam rubber.

For extra protection, body armor is recommended. Body armor is able to deflect the impact of an accident. Early body armor was heavy and uncomfortable. The latest designs, however, offer better protection and more comfort.

Body armor is made of a thin layer of hard plastic. It is backed by absorbent foam rubber. Body armor covers the shoulders, chest, back, elbows, and lower legs. Riders wear a T-shirt beneath their body armor. This prevents chafing and makes the ride more comfortable.

Many riders recommend wearing a good pair of motocross jeans. All motocross jeans are now made of nylon. The best have leather seats for added comfort. They also have a protective knee cap with a soft liner.

A good pair of jeans should last an entire motocross season. Avoid all-leather jeans. They are hot, heavy, expensive—and difficult to clean. Nylon jeans can be thrown into the washing machine.

The quality of gloves are often overlooked when riders select their gear. But when stones and other objects start flying, the importance of good gloves is suddenly realized.

A good pair of padded gloves is recommended.

Experts recommend gloves that have dense foam padding. Foam padding offers the best finger protection. Curved palms are also a good feature. They reduce blistering, and do not bunch when the rider grips the handlebar.

The best gloves are made of a synthetic material. They provide better gripping power in wet and muddy conditions. Their tight wrist bands prevent debris from entering the glove.

Finally, a thin, lightweight nylon jacket is recommended. A bulky race jacket is hot and won't allow a lot of free movement.

The number one rule for racing gear purchase is this: Think safety first. Buying colorful or fashionable gear might make you look good. But if the gear doesn't protect you, it is worthless.

The best safety gear of all is a fit and trim body. If you tire easily and become weak, the chances for an accident increase. Even more, a well-conditioned motocross rider has a much better chance of winning a race than someone who is out of shape. Exercise and eat right to keep yourself healthy and alert.

*A thin nylon jacket protects the driver
from mud and water.*

Learning to Motocross

Joining a club or motocross school is the best way to learn how to motocross. Many motocross manufacturers sponsor these clubs and schools. To find out where the nearest motocross club or school is to you, ask your local motocross bike dealer.

Before you can learn how to motocross race, you first must learn how to ride. The best place to practice is off of the road in a field.

Start on flat, straight ground. Sit stationary in first gear and ease out the clutch handle. Don't accelerate too quickly. Let the bike roll at a low speed. When you get your balance, put your feet up on the pegs and slowly turn the throttle.

Now you are ready for your first motocross lesson: How to use the brakes. It is important to remember not to lock up your brakes when you want to slow down. Locking your brakes will cause sudden stops—and possibly accidents.

First, brake the rear wheel only. Practice accelerating and braking repeatedly. Try to stop in a shorter distance without locking up the rear wheel. At the same time, shift your weight back. This will help you keep your balance, and shorten braking distance.

Locking the brakes can cause accidents.

Once you feel comfortable with the rear brake, test the powerful front brake. Roll your bike. Practice coming to a straight, even stop using the hand brake. Don't try to stop too quickly. Become familiar with the front brake before you attempt hard stops. If you don't, you may find yourself tumbling over the handlebars.

Now that you've mastered straight stops, practice braking during turns. Without practice, braking wheels can slide from under an inexperienced rider. Don't try braking in sharp turns just yet. Save this for later—when you've mastered the gradual turns.

Nothing beats a quick start.

While braking can get a rider safely through a race, nothing beats a quick start. In motocross, the best way to start is full throttle—spinning the rear wheel as quickly as possible. Though it sounds reckless, the reason is simple. Motocross engines run best at full power.

Getting off to a quick start is easy. Rev the engine to full speed, drop the clutch out all the way, and take off—keeping control of your bike. A quick start can mean the difference between winning and losing a race.

There's only one problem with a quick start: It creates a wheelie. And with your front wheel entirely off the ground, you run the risk of losing control of the bike.

To control the wheelie, put your weight forward as far as you can. Do it right away—before the wheel rises from the ground. Lean over the handlebars and push the wheel down. You won't be able to keep it completely down. But if the wheel only comes up one foot, you've done a great job—and you're off to a great start!

While controlling the wheelie, jab your boot toes into the dirt and use them as rudders. Otherwise, the rear wheel will fishtail out from under you. Once the bike grabs onto the track and roars off, shift your weight back into the seat.

But there is no time to relax. A good motocross rider rarely eases up on the accelerator. And there's a difficult course ahead. It takes much strength, determination, balance, and riding skill to conquer it.

Conquering the Motocross Track

The first curve in a motocross track is usually a long, sweeping turn. Some riders take this turn on the outer edge. But the best way to tackle it is on the inside. This gives you a perfect opportunity to pass the other riders.

Chances are, the next few turns won't be so easy. There will be tight turns, uphill and downhill turns—and even jump turns!

A tight turn makes you change direction and slow down. Try to keep the throttle up and stay off the brakes as long as you can. Then drop into a lower gear. This way, you can maintain power on the rear wheel throughout the turn.

In an uphill or downhill turn, drop into a lower gear. Then shift your weight toward the top of the hill to keep both wheels on the ground. At the same time, let your inside boot slide over the dirt. This will give you more balance and stability so you can make a tight turn—and pass the other riders.

The better you get at making tough, tight turns, the less you will use your brakes. The key is learning to shift your weight, using your boots for stabilization and balance, and taking advantage of the berm.

Tight turns are tricky.

Turning on a berm.

A berm is a ridge of packed dirt on the outer rim of a turn. If there is no one on the berm, use it for a quick turn. Come into it fast, ease up on the accelerator at the last possible moment, then turn your bike sideways into it. This will allow the front and back wheels to hit the berm at the same time. When this happens, turn up the throttle again. The bike will spring from the berm and zoom down the track.

Watch Out for the Whoop-De-Doos

The turns aren't the only obstacles you'll have to conquer on the motocross track. There are other devilish devices waiting to knock unsuspecting motocross riders from their bikes.

One of the most challenging are the whoop-de-doo bumps, also known as washboard roads. They are a series of bone-jarring depressions that often lie in the straightaways.

Your first reaction might be to take it slow over these bumps. But that just makes their impact even worse. Take the whoop-de-doo bumps at high speed. Get up on the foot pegs, bend your knees slightly, and shift your weight back. Your front and back wheels will skim over the tops of the bumps.

Jumps

Another common and difficult motocross obstacle is the jump. Jumps look scary because they make the bike leave the ground. But with proper technique and practice, jumps can be fun and exciting.

*With the proper technique and practice,
jumps can be exciting and fun.*

Ideally, keep as close to the ground as possible during all jumps. Land the rear wheel first and land moving away. Shift your weight back once you feel yourself becoming airborne. Then pull yourself forward so the rear wheel lands first. Make sure you power up the throttle before you land. This prevents the front wheel from slamming hard on the ground.

Typically, there are three kinds of jumps: horizontal, downhill, and uphill. Approach the horizontal jump with the throttle up. As soon as the rear wheel leaves the ground, close the throttle. Push from the handlebars, then throttle up once the rear wheel touches the ground. At the same time, pull yourself forward.

Approach the downhill jump with the power up—and keep it up the moment you are airborne. Close the throttle until just before you land, then open it again, keeping your weight forward as you touch ground.

The uphill jump is the trickiest to handle. That's because the front end of the bike is already up in the air. If you turn up the throttle, you might lose control.

Brake at the last moment you reach an uphill jump. Then go up the ramp at half speed. When your rear wheel reaches the edge, close the throttle and push yourself back. Throttle up only when the rear wheel is about to land.

Riding techniques change from track to track. But some basic rules never change:

•keep the power up whenever possible;

•don't brake until the last possible moment;

•keep the front wheel down.

And, of course, the more you practice, the better you will get. Stay in control of your bike at all times and you will get the most out of this fast-paced and exciting sport.

Falling

Motocross riding includes many turns and obstacles. Falling cannot be avoided. Knowing how to fall is just as important as riding techniques, and can prevent injury.

When you realize you are about to fall, try to get your arms and legs as close as you can to your body. Wrap your arms around your head. This reduces the chance of whiplash, and offers your head more protection.

Falling cannot be avoided.

At the same time, tuck your legs into your stomach. When you hit the ground, you will be wrapped up in a ball. This allows you to roll, which lessens the chance of injury.

Where to Race

Motocross tracks can be found all over the country. Some are formal, with starting gates, finish lines, and plenty of fans. Most are less formal. They are natural courses that can be found in any open country. Anyone with a motocross bike can direct you to these courses.

Motocross courses can be found all over the country.

Should you master these rural motocross courses, you may one day decide to join the Trans-AMA series. It was started in 1968, and is considered the top American motocross circuit. The most competitive motocross circuit is the International Grand Prix circuit. This is where the best motocross riders in the world race.

Whether you decide to race professionally or not, motocross offers all participants a thrilling and challenging sports activity. Stay in control, and you will find motocross a safe and rewarding sport as well.

For more information about motocross, write to:

Continental Motosport Club
P.O. Box 9458
San Bernardino, CA 92327

GLOSSARY

Alloy—a metal made by mixing two or more different metals and melting them together.

Berm—a dirt bank on a turn.

Full-faced helmet—a motocross helmet that has a face guard bolted on.

Lugs—small rubber knobbles on a motocross bike tire that give the tire its gripping power.

Motocross—cross-country motorcycling.

Rev—to increase the revolutions per minute on an engine; to drive at high speed.

Tear-off sheets—thin plastic sheets fitted to goggle lenses to protect the lenses from scratches and mud.

Wheelie—to ride with the front wheel off the ground.

Whiplash—an injury to the spine caused by a jerking motion of the head.

Whoop-de-doos—a series of bumps on a motocross course.